Lost In Chaos, Found In Dreams

Snehamsika Batchu

BookLeaf Publishing

India | USA | UK

Made with ❤ on the BookLeaf Publishing Platform
www.bookleafpub.in
www.bookleafpub.com

Dedication

To the quiet moments, the untold stories, and the
whispers of the heart—For those who find poetry in the
spaces between words,
who carry dreams in their silence,
and who see beauty in both the light and the shadows.

Preface

This book is a mess—of thoughts, of dreams, of the strange in-between where reality blurs and the mind runs wild. Some of these poems spilled out in moments of clarity, others in complete confusion. Either way, they refused to stay quiet.

If you've ever caught yourself lost in a daydream, overthinking a single moment, or unraveling thoughts that don't quite make sense—then you might find something familiar here. These words don't follow rules. They drift, collide, scatter, and settle, just like the mind does.

Read them in order, or don't. Let them sit with you, or let them slip away. Either way, welcome to the chaos.

Acknowledgements

This book wouldn't exist without the people who have shaped my life in ways big and small.
To my family—thank you for always believing in me, even when I wasn't sure of myself. Your love and support have been the quiet strength behind every word I write.
To my friends—you've listened to my endless thoughts, encouraged me when I hesitated, and reminded me why I love doing this. I'm so grateful for your presence, your patience, and the way you always show up.
To the Authors who have inspired me—your words have been my refuge, my guide, and my reminder that stories have the power to heal.
And to you, dear reader—thank you for being here. Whether you're just flipping through these pages or finding something that stays with you, I'm grateful for the time you're giving to these words. This book is as much yours as it is mine.

Love,
Hamsika

Held by Daydreams

I slip away in quiet dreams,
Where nothing's ever as it seems.
The world outside is loud and wild,
But here, I'm weightless—soft, beguiled.
The noise subsides, the rush slows down,
No heavy thoughts to pull me down.
In drifting moments, lost yet free,
Daydreams bring me back to me.

Echoes of Ourselves

Look at the passersby,
The cabs rush past, relentless,
A world in motion, chaotic.
Prime time for humans,
chasing after daily bread.

In this daily chase,
why do we feel the need to join?
Can't time pause, just for a moment,
so we can meet ourselves,
and learn to love who we are?

Breath of Gold

In stillness warm,
light cascades,
a golden dance through hidden glades.

Each breath, a spark,
each glance, a kiss,
the soul alight, dissolved in bliss.

The Battle Within

Heart says, *"Leap! Love! Feel!"*
Mind says, *"Wait. Think. Heal."*
Heart races toward the unknown,
Mind builds walls of stone.
"What if it's magic?" Heart pleads.
"What if it's ruin?" Mind concedes.
Heart aches for things unseen,
Mind clings to what has been.
I stand between them, lost in the fight,
Hoping one day, they'll both be right.

The Strength in Softness

They said strength is loud, unshaken, bold,
A clenched fist, a heart turned cold.
But I've seen power in quiet hands,
In steady love, in soft demands.
Strength is the voice that doesn't shout,
The one that stays when fear calls out.
It's bending, not breaking, knowing your worth,
Holding your ground with gentle words.
So call me soft, but don't mistake—
There's fire in the way I stay.

Flames of My Untamed Soul

I was never meant for quiet rooms,
for paths too neat, for measured tunes.
There's a fire in me that won't sit still,
a hunger that no silence kills.
I crave the rush of open skies,
the kind of life that terrifies.
I am not here to play it safe,
to shrink, to bow, to know my place.
Let me chase, let me burn,
let me live and never return.

The Fear of Never Being Enough

I have set myself against the impossible,
a version of me that doesn't break, doesn't fail—
a distant star I'll never reach,
but still, I chase.
I measure myself in borrowed words,
in glances held a second too long,
in the silence after I speak—
waiting, always waiting.
I have chased approval like a ghost,
tried to fill spaces I was never meant to fit.
No matter how much I give,
there is always more I should have been.
What if I am only almost?
What if I am always just close?
I shrink, I rise, I break, I mend,
but the doubt lingers—
a shadow I cannot outrun.

Whispers

I have told my secrets to the night,
let the wind carry my quiet hopes.
I have whispered dreams to distant stars,
wishing they'd burn them into fate.
Some nights, they flicker back at me,
as if to say, *we're listening.*
Other nights, they stay silent,
and I wonder if I asked for too much.
But still, I whisper, still, I hope—
because somewhere in the dark,
I know they are waiting.

Breaking Shackles

They told me who to be before I could choose,
wrapped me in rules I never made.
"You should be quiet."
"You must be kind."
"You should stay small."
"You must not mind."
I have swallowed their words like bitter seeds,
but I am done growing into their shape.
I was not meant to fit their mold,
to shrink, to bend, to do as told.
So I unlearn, I unravel, I break—
until I am nothing but my own.

Bed of Roses

"Her life is a bed of roses,"
They said.
Vibrant and beautiful.
But can they see?
It's not the roses— It's me who makes it look effortless,
Wonderful, and full of glee.
Seriously,
Can you see all the trouble those roses gave me?
The pain, the scars— I made them look like glittering
stars.
I'm a girl, you say,
"Life is a bed of roses for you,"
"Everyone wants such a comfortable life."
Do you realise?
With the roses came the thorns.
It's me again—not the roses!
It's me who makes this **bed of roses** seem so bewitching,
So enchanting,
That the thought of it fills you with envy.
It's not the roses— **It's me!**

The Art of Breaking and Rebuilding

I have shattered more times than I can count,
watched pieces of me slip through my hands,
tried to hold on, tried to stay whole—
but some things are meant to fall apart.
I have learned to sit with the wreckage,
to trace the cracks, to name the ruins.
Not everything broken is lost.
Not everything lost needs finding.
So I gather what's left,
shape myself from the dust,
build something new—
something stronger,
something mine.

Mondays!

I wake up ready to conquer the day,
then remember—it's Monday. No way.
The emails glare, the meetings loom,
my soul sighs, *please, not another Zoom.*
Coffee helps, but only a bit,
by noon, I'm just a caffeinated mess of regret.
But the worst part? The weekend tease—
where does it go? Who hit fast-forward on peace?

Leafy Conundrum

I stare at the vegetables, full of intent,
I'll eat healthy this week—I'm 100%...
But then cheese calls my name, so does cake,
surely self-care is more important than kale?
I buy both, pretend it's balanced,
and ignore the spinach rotting in silence.

Adult Much?!

I pay my bills, I cook (sometimes),
Yet adulting still feels like crimes.
Should I own a house? Invest in stocks?
Or just survive these mental blocks?
I google "how to file tax returns,"
End up watching a cat who learns.
My fridge holds sauces, nothing real,
I guess that's *meal prep,* what a steal.
I wear blazers to feel profound,
But trip on stairs and crash right down.
If life's a test, I'm on my own,
When do we get *grown-up zone?*

Anti Social

I make plans with joy, full of cheer,
Then dread them as the date draws near.
I said I'd go, I *should* be there,
But my couch is *so* unfair.
What if I cancel? What if I stay?
My phone's on silent—hope fades away.
But I force myself, I show up bright,
And laugh like I had *planned this night.*
Then next day, my energy's gone,
I'll need a week to *carry on.*
I love my friends, but here's the twist—
Can we just *exist* via text list?

Midnight Crisis

I should be sleeping, drifting away,
But my brain has other games to play.
"Are you behind?" it asks real slow,
"Where's your success? What do you *know*?"
Should I be married? Should I have land?
Am I too late or just *too bland*?
I spiral, I scroll, I overthink,
Then suddenly, I need a drink.
Maybe life's just one big scam,
None of us *actually* have a plan.
By sunrise, I still don't know,
But slap on a smile and just go.

17. Mess

High-rise jeans, a rebel's stance,
Messy hair, a fleeting dance.
Tailored suits, a power pose,
Glammed-up dresses, grace bestows.
A vision painted, bold and bright,
A walking dream in city lights.
But deep within, a tempest sways,
A tangled storm of yesterdays.
Who would guess beneath the sheen,
Lies a world both fierce and keen?
A mind that races, wild, untamed,
A heart with fires yet unnamed.
Perfection's veil, a clever guise,
Hiding truths behind her eyes.
She walks in light, she drowns in dark,
A paradox, a work of art.

Email Wars

Inbox full, my patience thin,
Each "kind regards" a tiny sin.
"Circle back," "Let's sync soon,"
Do they plan *to haunt my room?*
"Following up!" Oh, the nerve,
Can I please just *swerve?*
The email chain—a cursed loop,
My sanity slips, bit by scoop.
One-click, delete, escape in sight,
But *somehow*, they reply at night.
A war I'll never truly win,
Yet here I go—reply again.

Joy of Cancelled plans

An invite comes, I hesitate,
Social pressure seals my fate.
I dress up, I push through,
Then—*a message* comes in view.
"Plans changed, let's reschedule soon!"
Oh, sweet relief, like a silver moon.
Suddenly, the night is mine,
Sweatpants on, I *sip my wine.*
I love my friends, I truly do,
But sometimes, peace deserves its due.

Burning the Blueprint

I held on till my knuckles turned white,
Chained myself to versions of me that no longer fit.
Called it duty, called it strength,
Refused to see the weight of it.
But time is ruthless—it bends, it sways,
It pries open fists that beg to stay.
Some dreams collapse to build new ground,
Some battles end so you can be *found.*
Not every road is mine to claim,
Not every fall is wrapped in shame.
What breaks, what shifts, what drifts away,
Might just be clearing the way.
So I unclench my grip, I let the tide turn,
Not everything lost is reason to mourn.
I trust what remains, I step into the free,
And what's meant for me will rise **with me**

A Place so Familiar

Ever sat in a room that knew your name,
where laughter swirled, warm and bright,
yet somehow, you were *elsewhere*,
a ghost in your own life?
The voices move around you,
but none seem to land.
You nod, you smile, you play along,
but the edges never soften.
And then, one day, in a place unknown,
where no one waits, no one asks,
you step outside, breathe it in,
and somehow, you just *belong*.
No bending, no shrinking, no act to maintain—
just air that doesn't question you.
Maybe home isn't a place you chase,
but one that *recognises you first*.